WHEN YOUR LOVED ONE DIES

"...the time of my departure is at hand..."
2 Timothy 4:6 (KJV)

A Practical Funeral Preparation Guide For Family Members

Second Edition

Samuel W. Hale, Jr.

Copyright © 2000
Samuel W. Hale, Jr.
100 Radcliff Road
Springfield, Illinois 62703
217-585-4154
Swhalejr@AOL.com

* * *

All rights reserved.
No part of this publication may be reproduced,
stored in a retrieval system,
or transmitted in any form,
or by any means
(electronic, photocopy, recording, etc.)
without the written permission of the author.

* * *

Printed in the U.S.A.
by
Morris Publishing
3212 E. Hwy 30
Kearney, NE 68847
800-650-7888

* * *

1st Printing, August, 2000
2nd Edition, March, 2002

* * *

LOC: 00-91195
ISBN: 0-9703638-0-X

Cover Photography
Copyright © 1997 by Morris Press

When Your Loved One Dies,
the Surviving Spouse and Family Members
are faced with some startling discoveries
which, if not dealt with properly, can cause some
frightening and frustrating moments long before,
and after, the Final Farewells to their Loved One
shall have been expressed.

This Guide offers some Practical and Important
Information and Suggestions
to Bereaving Family Members
who have the Challenging Responsibilities
of making the Funeral Arrangements for a Loved One;
of Settling that Loved Ones' Affairs;
and also of assisting other Family Members
as they confront and adjust to their Loved Ones'
Death.

* * *

TABLE OF CONTENTS

Introduction   v

Chapter 1 - The Place of Death
At Home   1
At the Hospital   2
In A Nursing Home   3
Other   4

Chapter 2 - Informing Family Members
Immediate Family   5
Extended Family   6
In-Laws   6
Close Friends & Others   6

Chapter 3 - Contacting a Funeral Home
The Loved One's Preference   9
You Must Decide   9
Removing the Body   10
Scheduling an Appointment   10
    Cremate or Not
    Selecting a Casket
    Confirming the Itemized Fee Schedule
    Arrangements for Paying the Funeral Costs
    Securing Death Certificates
    Selecting the Burial Clothing
    Parting Views

Chapter 4 - The Pastor's Role
Comforting the Family Members   17
Advising with Decision Making   18
Planning the Order of Service   18
Clearing Arrangements for the Funeral   19
    At the Church
    At the Funeral Home
    At the Grave Site

Contents

    After the Interment
    Compensating the Pastor

Chapter 5 - Gathering Information
    Personal Documents   21
        Will
        Designated Executor
        Personal Attorney
        Final Instructions
        Cemetery Plot
        Pre-Need Arrangements
        Birth Certificate
        Social Security #
        Marriage Certificate
        Divorce Decree
        Adoption Papers
    Financial Information   23
        Bank Accounts
        Safety Deposit Boxes
        Investments
        Creditors/Outstanding Debts
        Credit Cards
        Tax Information
        Mortgage Papers
    Military Records   27
        Serial #
        V.A. Claim #
        G.I. Insurance #
    Employer Information   27
        Retirement Information
        Pension Plans
        Group Life/Health Insurance Plans
        Accrued Vacation/Sick Pay
        Credit Union Balances

Contents

Personal Insurance Policies   28
Other Documents   28
Special Requests   28

Chapter 6 - Preparing for the Funeral
Counseling with the Pastor   29
Confirming the Date & Time   29
Visitation With the Family   30
Contacting Family Members   30
Writing the Obituary   30
Selecting the Right Photograph(s)   31
Confirming Family Participants   31
Selecting the Family Floral Spray   32
Memorial Tributes in Lieu of Flowers   32
Confirming the Family Assembly Place   32
Picking Up Arriving Family Members   33
Confirming Lodging Arrangements   33
Confirming Family Car Designations   33
    Who Is In The Family Car(s)?
    Who Will Be Driving Other Cars?
    Who Will Be Riding in Which Car?
Identifying the Funeral Cars   34
Providing for Family Meals   35
Proper Funeral Attire   35

Chapter 7 - Taking Care of Business
Contacting Legal Counsel   37
Contacting Banks/Financial Institutions   37
Contacting the Social Security Office   37
Contacting the Veteran's Administration   38
Contacting Insurance Companies   38
Paying Outstanding Debts   39
Thanking Those Who Remembered   39
Providing for Those Who Remain   40
Securing a Headstone Marker   41

Contents

Chapter 8 - Facing the Future
Putting Your Own Affairs In Order	43
Keeping Your Will Updated	43
Establish A Pre-Arrangement Plan	43
Keeping In Contact With Your Relatives	44
Keeping In Contact With Your Friends	45

Chapter 9 - Strengthening Your Spiritual Affairs
Reviewing Your Spiritual Life Style	47
Setting Your House In Order	50

Chapter 10 - Other Scriptures For These Moments
The Biblical View of Death	53
God's Assurance for Your Strength	55
The Best Is Yet To Come	56

Appendices
Obituary Format	61
Personal Information Inventory	67
Family Seating Order	76
Funeral Home Service Charges	78
Funeral Planning Check List	79
Suggested Orders of Service	81
At The Church or Funeral Home	
At The Gravesite	
Special Notes	82
Wakes/Visitations With The Family	
Memorial Observations of Fraternal Organizations	
Military Ceremonies	

# # #

INTRODUCTION

"It just happened so suddenly!"

"I never thought she would die so young."

"But, he just went to the Doctor's last week..."

"I wonder who's going to take care of the Children?"

"But we can't afford that priced Casket!"

"Momma deserves the **Best!**"

"But she said she was going to give **Me** that set of China!"

"Will? What Will?"

"Junior, when are **You** going to finish paying for **Your** Part of the Funeral Expenses?"

* * *

Perhaps **YOU** have heard some of these Statements being made in reference to the Death of some Friend or Loved One. Be it expected, sudden, or tragic, Death can be a most Frightening and Frustrating Experience for the Family Members. Inevitably, these and many other concerns, confront every Family at the Death of a Loved One. Many of them can be resolved **before** that Moment of Death Comes!

This **Practical Guide** is intended to help **You** and **Your Family through** the process of Dealing with the many Elements and Issues that the Death of a Loved One may present.

Introduction

As You read this Guide may You be Enlightened, Comforted, Helped, Directed, Strengthened, and Challenged to help Your Family meaningfully deal with, prepare for, and carry out the Funeral Arrangements of Your Loved One. May You also be challenged to properly and effectively help Your Family Members be better able to accept and adjust to the Moment when You become the Loved One to be Funeralized. And may You also seek the Guidance, Strength, and Presence of the Holy Spirit to help You through each of You daily encounters.

* * *

Chapter 1
The Place of Death

One of the first encounters with the Death of a Loved One occurs at the location in which that person actually dies. Sometimes it is at Home, or in the Hospital or Nursing Home, or at the Scene of an Accident. In either case, you will have to face various persons and situations which may bring additional trauma to you and/or to other Relatives and Friends present at that moment. It is our prayer that the following suggestions might help you through those moments.

At Home

When the Death of Your Loved One occurs **At Home**, several situations may come to bear. Often that Loved One may have been ill over a period of time. If so, the Family may have been expecting this moment to come. Even in that case, the hopes that **this is NOT that moment** may still be in the minds of some Members and Friends present. **The reality that this IS that moment MUST be accepted and dealt with!**

In a matter of moments the Home will be crowded with more people. The Paramedics may be called. The Police may have to be involved, especially in the case of suspected foul play, or uncertainty of the cause of Death. Soon Neighbors, Friends, and other Relatives may arrive, and the House will rapidly undergo a transformation as you seek to accommodate those who have arrived. This may prove to become rather chaotic.

In these moments **it is very important** to make sure that important papers, personal belongings, and valuables are **kept out of sight!** You must realize that the security of the Home is compromised in moments such as this.

The Place of Death

In the event that it is necessary to transport the Loved One to the Hospital, unless a trusted Family Member or Friend can be left behind, the Home should be locked until You return.

At the Hospital

When Your Loved One dies **At the Hospital**, although the setting may be different, some of the same experiences may be encountered. In this setting, the room may be filled with Relatives and Close Friends. Numerous Hospital Staff may be coming and going. In many cases Relatives of the other Patient(s) in the room may be present. And in some cases You may be in the Emergency Room area. In either case it is most important that You and the Family Members allow the Nursing Staff to carry out their responsibilities. Another room or area may be designated for the Family Members to gather until the Doctor is able to talk to the Family. It is important that proper decorum be kept by **ALL**.

As soon as is possible, Your Loved One's Pastor should be contacted, if he is not already present, just as at the **Home**, Your Loved One's Personal Property should be gathered and kept for safety purposes. Often those items may already be secured at the Nurses Station, or some designated area in the Hospital. Be sure to inquire of the Nursing Staff, if You are unsure. Some close Family Member should also be prepared to confirm with the Hospital Staff the Mortuary Service to be contacted. Usually, local calls can be made from the designated Waiting Area to inform other Family Members and Friends of Your Loved One's Death. Although such calls may be free, care ought be taken to only make those calls which are immediately necessary. Long distance calls should be made at Home, or on someone's personal cell phone.

The Place of Death

When talking with the Doctor, You may be asked various questions about your Loved One's previous health condition. You should also be prepared to decide whether an Autopsy is desired. Be sure You understand the circumstances and causes of the Death of Your Loved One as much as can be determined. Some causes may be hereditary, and thus affect other Members of the Family! The Hospital Staff will also need to know whether your Loved One was an Organ Donor.

As soon as is possible, prepare to leave the Hospital as quietly as possible. Thank the Nursing Staff for their assistance and service.

In A Nursing Home

In the event that Your Loved One Dies in a **Nursing Home** or **Health Care Facility**, the situation may be quite similar to that of a Hospital setting. However, there will be distinct differences. Usually the Nursing Home Staff will not be prepared to render the type of Emergency Care that would be expected at a Hospital. In many cases a Paramedic Team may have been called. And depending upon the time of day in which the Death occurs, the hallways may be impeded by elderly residents, some of whom may not be fully conscious of, or focused on, what has happened to Your Loved One.

Still care ought be taken to follow many of the same steps and procedures taken for the Home or Hospital. Be prepared to confirm any Directives on File with the Nursing Home; to contact Your Loved One's Pastor, if he is not already present; to confirm and secure Your Loved One's Personal Property from the Nursing Home; to confirm whether an Autopsy is desired; to confirm contact with the preferred Mortuary Service; and to contact other Family Members and Friends. As soon as is possible the Family should retire to one of the Family Member's Homes to address needed concerns and planning.

The Place of Death

Other

Sometimes Death may come to Your Loved One in some other setting. You may be called to the scene of an accident, or some other tragedy. As traumatic as such moments may be, it is important that many of the previously mentioned concerns still be followed.

At such times, care should be taken to secure Your Loved One's Personal Property at the scene, and to provide what ever information whcih mat be requested by the Authorities on the scene. Contact Your Pastor and/or Your Loved One's Pastor as soon as possible. He and other Family Members and Friends may be summoned to the Hospital where previously acknowledged arrangements will still need to be made.

* * *

Chapter 2
Informing Family Members

The shock and trauma of the Death of Your Loved One no doubt will not be over before You will have to contact other Family Members and inform them what has happened. As the old adage goes, "**It's a tough job to be done, but somebody's got to do it.**" Right now the burden may fall upon You! If that becomes the case, then there are some important facts to remember and to carry out.

Immediate Family

This may be one of the hardest tasks to perform. This group will include the Spouse, Children, Mother, Father, Brothers, and Sisters. It may also include divorced, separated, incarcerated, and even hospitalized Family Members. It may include Children away in school or in the Armed Services. In either case they need to be informed. In the event of Family Members in the Armed Services, the Red Cross is most efficient in reaching, informing, and even assisting that Family Member in getting home for the Funeral when possible.

Family Members who are incarcerated usually are not able to be released. Yet in some cases, they may be allowed to have a private viewing prior to the scheduled Funeral. Contact should be made with the Facility where that Family Member is incarcerated.

Contacting the other Immediate Family Members is essential, not only to inform them of their Loved One's Death, but also to confirm their anticipated time and method of arrival. In the case of the Children away in school, plans may also have to be made for their transportation home.

Informing Family Members

A similar need may also exist for Elderly Members of the Family desiring to attend the Funeral. Try to limit the cost of phone calls by asking certain Family Members in various areas of the Country to inform the Family Members in their area and to confirm their anticipated time and method of arrival. Try to have as much information confirmed when calling.

Extended Family

Inevitably, the list of Cousins, and Aunts, and Uncles, and Grandparents, and Great-grandparents begins to grow over the years. Some of these persons may be unable to come, but they need to be informed! Again utilize the "**phone tree**" approach in contacting this group of Family Members as well. As You can see, the cost of Informing the Family Members can become quite expensive. But every effort ought be made as much as is possible.

In-Laws

If You are not careful, this group of Family Members can be easily and tragicly overlooked, especially if there has been limited contact between them and the surviving Spouse. Care must be taken here because there is still a direct relationship between the In-Laws and the Children of the Deceased. Those relationships must be properly maintained, at least for the Children's sake. The In-Laws may be the most logical and capable persons to assist in the care of surviving Children. And sometimes the In-Law Relationship may seem more like Blood Relatives. In either case, make sure that the In-Laws are informed.

Close Friends & Others

Sometimes Close Friends are privy to more information about the Deceased than many Immediate Family Members are.

Informing Family Members

In other cases, the Friendship has engendered itself even to other Family Members. As a matter of fact, these persons may seem like Family. They may be former classmates, employees, childhood friends, members of mutual organizations, and even ex-boy friends and girl-friends. In respect to the Friendship of those persons and Your Loved One, make sure they are informed!

* * *

"Let all things be done decently and in order."

- 1 Corinthians 14:40 (KJV)

Chapter 3
Contacting a Funeral Home

You may not be over the initial shock of the Death of your Loved One, however, given procedures necessitate contacting some Funeral Home for Mortuary Services to be performed. Again some serious decisions must be made. What do you tell the Hospital Staff? What Funeral Home comes to mind?

The Loved One's Preference

More and more people are making decisions such as this before they die. Some have already made out Wills or Statements of Final Wishes to address this and other matters. It is most important that You seek to confirm if Your Loved One has enacted such documents so that You will be in compliance with their wishes. Even if no such Document exists, seek to determine if any of the Family Members are aware of a Funeral Home preference of Your Loved One.

Many persons have entered into "Pre-Need" Programs with Funeral Homes. These programs are actually insurance programs designed to assure the Deceased and relieve the Family of such crucial decisions at a trying time. "Pre-Need" programs are legal arrangements in which the Deceased has made provisions for their Funeral Arrangements. The casket has already been selected. The price range for the Funeral costs have already been determined. And in most cases, the Funeral Home has already been determined.

You Must Decide

Whatever the circumstances, now is the time to confirm the selection of a Funeral Home.

Contacting a Funeral Home

Usually the Hospital or Nursing Home Staff will seek that information prior to your leaving the facilities. This is important because the bed and room must be prepared for other patients. Life goes on! As soon as is possible, consult with the Family Members responsible and confirm your decision to the Hospital or Nursing Home Staff.

Removing the Body

Wherever Your Loved One's Death occurred, the time will soon come when the Funeral Home Staff will come to **remove the Body**. This will be another traumatic moment. There is a sense of finality in this process. But there are some important facts to be remembered and observed.

Make sure that rings, jewelry, and personal items are removed from the Body and given to someone responsible. Use discretion in allowing smaller children to witness this process. The same is true with other Members of the Family who may be highly emotional. Although this is a sobering and traumatic moment for You and the Family, the Funeral Home Staff have some legal and professional obligations to follow. Help them do their job by giving them adequate space and assistance as may be requested.

Scheduling an Appointment

Before the Funeral Home Staff leaves the premises, seek to confirm the day and time to meet with a Representative to discuss the Funeral Arrangements. When that time comes, be sure that the responsible Family Members (Spouse, immediate Family Members, Person having Power of Attorney) are included and present at that meeting.

Contacting a Funeral Home

During the Meeting with the Funeral Home Staff be sure that You understand that Staff's procedures, as well as their Fees! Now is the time to clarify any concerns about the Family's Obligations to the Funeral Home. Be sure to address the following matters:

Cremate or Not? - More and more Family Members are opting to cremate for various reasons - some religious, some financial, and some just personal. If this is a consideration for Your Loved One, then certain facts should be realized.

First, the Cremation process can be done prior to or following the Funeral Service. In the event that You choose to Cremate **before** the scheduled Service, then You will be encouraged to select an Urn, or some type of container in which to place the Ashes of Your Loved One. This Container may be on display during the Service, and You may choose to bury it in a Grave, or in a Crypt where Family Members can occasionally visit and show their respects.

You should also be aware that the Cremation costs may also include the purchase of a special Cremation Casket which will also be included in the Cremation process. Some Funeral Homes may rent Display Caskets in which Your Loved One will be placed during the Funeral Service prior to the Cremation process. In those cases the inner linings of the Casket are disposed of after the Services.

As much as is possible and practical, follow the Directives of Your Loved One, and strive to keep the concerns particularly of the Immediate Family in mind.

Contacting a Funeral Home

Selecting a Casket - You will be shown a variety of caskets on display. Often the more ornate and expensive caskets may be at the front of the display area. The price of Caskets vary, not only with the style and design, but more specifically with the material out of which it is made. Certain wooden caskets are much more expensive than steel caskets.

Steel caskets come in grades called gauges, and the price and quality varies with the gauges of steel used. Also the casket price may vary based on the type of seal that is used around the top. These seals are designed to prevent moisture from entering the Casket once it is permanently closed.

You should also keep in mind that, in most states, the law requires the casket to be placed in some type of container or "vault" in the grave. Usually these vaults are concrete. But some Families have chosen bronze or other metal vaults for this purpose. **Again Your choice also affects the Funeral Costs!**

Be cautious about selecting a casket solely based on looks! The prudent Family is cautious about how much money is literally placed **"in the ground"**. Remember, there will be other outstanding debts and expenses to be met.

Confirming the Itemized Fee Schedule - When the Family's decision is made about the choice of casket, the Family Cars for the Funeral Procession, and whatever other amenities provided by the Funeral Home, **be sure to secure an Itemized Fee Schedule** showing the costs for each service rendered by the Funeral Home. This information should help determine the amount to be expended on the Funeral of Your Loved One.

Contacting a Funeral Home

If necessary, insist on the **Itemized Fee** prior to finalizing instructions to the Funeral Home to avoid any misunderstandings about specific Services to be rendered.

Arrangements for Paying the Funeral Costs - In most cases the Funeral Home Staff will seek to confirm the Arrangements to be taken for paying the projected Funeral Costs for Your Loved One. This is all the more reason to be frugal in the determination of the decisions made for "**putting Your Loved One away**". Keep in mind that the Funeral Home is a **business**! Their job is to provide the Family with the "**best that money can buy**". However, they are also very much concerned about the Family's ability to pay for what they buy. This is all the more reason for discretion.

Many times the Funeral Home may seek assurances, or assignment of Life Insurance Policies, down payments, or even full payments of certain items, **before** they finalize their Funeral Services. Heaven only knows the number of Families who have made commitments in moments of grief that their resources could not match. Avoid putting Your Family and the Memory of Your Loved One in that kind of situation.

Securing Death Certificates - The Death of Your Loved One places some legal restrictions on the Family. Proof of Death is normally required before access to certain Financial Resources can be made. This includes Insurance Policies, Social Security Benefits, Veterans Benefits, Annuities, and other Employment Benefits. Be sure to request enough Official Copies of the Death Certificate as may be needed to facilitate the processing of these Resources.

Contacting a Funeral Home

Selecting the Burial Clothing - Some time prior to the Funeral the Funeral Home Staff will need certain Clothing items in which to bury Your Loved One. Again discretion ought be used in this matter as well. Think twice before purchasing **new** clothes for this occasion. An additional expense in this area may be the need for the services of a beautician. Sometimes the Funeral Home Staff has someone who normally provides this service. Otherwise, there may be someone that the Family prefers to provide that service. Be sure You are clear when these items or services are needed or are to be performed.

Parting Views - This Practice can be one of the most traumatic and trying moments for the Family Members. Often, because of past practice, some Family Members may assume that this procedure **has** to be included at the close of the Funeral Service.

In reality, that might be the **least** advisable time. Actually, the **most** opportune time to have the **Parting View** of Your Loved One is at the Close of the Visitation Period, and/or just before the Funeral Service begins. At that time the Family and Friends shall have viewed the Body and shall have taken their seats for the Funeral Service.

Closing of the Casket at that time allows a Sense of Closure to the Moment. The Biblical Focus of the Funeral is to direct the Family and Friends to see God's Hand and Plan in the Homegoing of Your Loved One. From that Time on, attention is directed from the Physical to the Spiritual.

Leaving the Casket open during the Service and/or Reopening the Casket at the Close of the Service conflicts with the Spiritual Purpose of the Funeral. It also imposes additional and needless stress on those who are still adjusting to the Loss of Your Loved One.

Contacting a Funeral Home

It will also increase the time frame of the Funeral Service. This could present additional problems when the Cemetery Staff is expecting the Burial Service to take place at a specified time.

By all means, confirm this matter with the Pastor!

* * *

"And I will give you pastors according to mine heart, which shall feed you with knowledge and understanding."

- Jeremiah 3:15 (KJV)

Chapter 4
The Pastor's Role

In the midst of all that is transpiring one of the most important, but often forgotten, steps to be taken is **contacting Your Loved One's Pastor!** On far too many occasions Families have proceeded with planning the Funeral Arrangements without first informing their Loved One's Pastor of the Death.

But the Pastor plays a most important Role to the Family in these moments. In most cases he has already interacted with the Hospital Staff and Funeral Homes Staff in similar situations. He is aware of the many types of decisions and circumstances that Family Members undergo and face at these times. His counsel and presence can be a rewarding Blessing to the Family. You would be most wise in contacting the Pastor as soon as possible, especially when the Family Members have been called to the bedside of a dying Loved One.

The Pastor can be most helpful in the following ways:

Comforting the Family Members

The experience of Death strikes people in different ways. Most experienced Pastors have already encountered many of those responses. He is conscious of the fact that his Presence, his Words of Comfort, and his Prayers can do so much in easing the tensions, anger, hurt, frustrations, and expressions of despondency resulting from the Death of Your Loved One. His efforts to direct the Family's Attention to God's Wisdom and Will in this moment can relieve so many emotions of the moment.

The Pastor's Role

In all honesty, You should also be aware of any strained relations or feelings that Your Loved One may have had for the Pastor. Usually he is already aware of them, but he is also committed to assist the Bereaved Family **through** this trying experience.

Advising with Decision Making

Since the Pastor has already dealt with various Health Care Staff persons and Funeral Home Staff persons, he usually is aware of their practices and procedures. He can be very valuable in helping the Family address various concerns with these persons as they negotiate the Arrangements.

Most Pastors realize that the ultimate decisions will be made by the Family. His Role is simply to help them be aware of the many factors that might affect and result from their decisions. Many of those factors can help facilitate the speed and efficiency of resolving many of the business matters to be addressed at this time.

Planning the Order of Service

When the Pastor and the Church are being considered for the Funeral Service, You must realized that You are talking about a Worship Experience! And since that is the case, it is the Pastors' specific responsibility and duty to **oversee** and **coordinate** the **Order of Service**. Any requests for persons to participate in the Service or items to be included in the Service should be cleared with and approved by the Pastor. Most Funeral Homes will provide a Clergy person to handle the Service at the Funeral Home when the Deceased is not affiliated with a Church. Even then certain procedures will be followed which comply with that establishment's policies. Keep in mind that such services by the Funeral Home will also be added to the Funeral expenses.

Clearing Arrangements for the Funeral

Part of the Pastor's Role also includes determining an appropriate Date and Time for the Funeral Services. Various factors will affect these decisions.

At the Church - When the Funeral is held at the Church numerous persons must be contacted in order to make the Family's experience as uplifting as possible. The Custodian must be informed to assure the facilities being properly cleaned and prepared for the Service. The Music Ministry must be informed so that appropriate music, instrumental and vocal can be provided. The Church Secretary must be informed so that accurate information about the Funeral can be disseminated to those inquiring about the Arrangements; and that provisions can be made for floral arrangements to be delivered; and that the Funeral Program can be prepared in sufficient time. The Church Clerk must be informed so that appropriate responses from the Church can be prepared for the Funeral. The Culinary Committee must be informed so that adequate provisions can be made for refreshments for the Family following the Interment. All of these situations should be cleared through and coordinated by the Pastor.

At the Funeral Home - Even when the Funeral Service is held at the Funeral Home, the Pastor is still accountable for seeing that many of those same Arrangements normally provided at the Church would still be provided at the Funeral Home.

At the Grave Site - In the event that the Family decides to hold the Funeral at the **Grave Site**, the Pastor, or some one designated from the Funeral Home, will be responsible for the **Grave Side Services**, whatever that may include. In most cases, these Services will focus primarily on the Committal of the Body into the Grave.

The Pastor's Role

In the event that Your Loved One is a Veteran, a local Veterans' Honor Guard and Burial Detail may provide Final Respects to their Fallen Comrade. In such case, the Pastor still has the responsibility to affirm the Biblical Message of Hope and Assurance for the Eternal Future of Your Loved One in those Final Moments.

After the Interment - When the Interment, the Committal of the Body, has been completed and the Family leaves the Grave Site, often the Family will return to the Church, or another designated place for Refreshments. This is one of the Pastor's and the Church's last opportunities to Minister to Your Bereaved Family.

Compensating the Pastor - In most cases the Pastor does not charge a fee for his Services. He usually considers his Services to Your Family as part of his Pastoral Ministry. Your Family, however, may wish to present him with a personal Expression of Appreciation for his Ministry to the Family. Such expression should be at the discretion of the Family.

* * *

Chapter 5
Gathering Information

The Death of a Loved One can present one of the most frustrating moments for an unprepared Family. It is for this very reason that it is wise to begin some of this process now! Almost immediately, after the Death of Your Loved One the need and search for Important Documents begins. Hospital or Emergency Personel may ask about Medications that Your Loved One may have been taking. The Funeral Home Staff will want to know about Insurance Policies and Financial resources for payment. Family Members will wonder about Wills and Your Loved One's Plans for Distribution of Property. All kinds of information will be needed to finalize Your Loved One's Affairs.

It would be wisdom to make copies of all Personal Documents, keeping one set of said copies in a safe place at home and the originals or another set in a Safe Deposit Box at the Bank. As soon as is possible and feasible, You should seek to secure and confirm the following Documents and Information:

Personal Documents

Will - This is perhaps one of the most important Documents to retrieve at the Death of Your Loved One. Many Legal, Practical, and Procedural Factors hinge on what has been written in a Will. Look for information that indicates a Lawyer whom Your Loved One may have secured. Copies may be placed in a Lock Box at the Bank or in some file, folder, box, under a mattress, or in some other container used for safe keeping.

Above all, BE SURE about the existance, or non-existance, of a Will BEFORE proceding with major plans for the Funeral, or for the Distribution of Your Loved One's Estate.

Gathering Information

Then follow the instructions of that Will to the letter to avoid Legal recourses of other Loved Ones, Family Members, and/or Creditors.

Designated Executor - Normally, the Will would clarify who is to carry out the Final Wishes of Your Loved One. That person is usually called the **Executor**.

In some cases the Executor may be the Lawyer retained to draw up the Will. In other cases he may be a Family Member or Friend. In either case, that person is to follow the Instructions of the Will as best as is feasible and legally practical.

Personal Attorney - Sometimes Your Loved One's Personal Attorney may be needed to assist in the Legal matters concerning Your Loved One's Affairs. Be sure to contact that person as soon as possible.

Final Instructions - In the event that a Will is not existant, Your Loved One may have left certain **Final Instructions**, written or verbal, which were intended to guide the Family at this point in time. Seek to make sure that any **Verbal Instructions** are **mutually** agreed upon by Family Members who may be privy to them. These Instructions may include the Distribution of Personal Items and Property, Bank Accounts, Payment of Bills, etc. In respect to Your Loved One, these **Final Instructions** may be just as important as a **Will**.

Cemetery Plot - In that bundle of "**papers**" may be found some information about a **Cemetery Plot** that Your Loved One may have purchased, or may be entitled to. This is especially true when a Spouse has predeceased Your Loved One. This is also true for Veterans and their spouses. Contacting the nearest V.A. Office should help to clarify this matter.

Gathering Information

If there is no Record of such transaction, be prepared to address this matter with the Funeral Home Staff. Usually there will be an additional Fee for the "opening and closing" of the Grave Site.

Pre-Need Arrangements - More and more Elderly persons are securing **Pre-Need Arrangements**. These are simply plans made to secure and confirm Funeral Arrangements with a Funeral Home prior to ones demise. These Arrangements usually include the selection of a Casket, and the specific Services to be rendered by the Funeral Home. Confirm with the respective Company whether these Arrangements have been fully paid for. Some unexpected problems can result if Your Loved One started on such a Plan and failed to complete the transactions or payments.

Personal Records - In many cases various other Documents or **Personal Records** may be needed to transact Business for Your Loved One. Once they are retrieved and secured you may need them for Your Loved One's Affairs. These Documents include: the **Birth Certificate**, the **Social Security Card and Number**, **Marriage Certificate(s)**, **Divorce Decree(s)**, and **Adoption Papers**. These Documents may be important factors in the execution of the **Will** or **Final Instructions**.

Financial Information

How much Your Loved One left will be a major concern for many of the Family, Friends, and Acquaintances - even **YOU!** Regardless of whose business it really is, the confirmation of this Information will be a major determining factor as to what to do for the Funeral, the outstanding bills, and the well-being of the Family Members who are left.

Gathering Information

Care should be taken discreetly to secure and address this matter. In many cases the **Will** or **Final Instructions** will indicate **who** is authorized to handle this procedure.

Bank Accounts - In the event that any of the Bank Accounts are in "**Joint Tenancy**", care should be taken to **withdraw** an adequate amount of "**operating cash**" as soon as possible. Various State Laws will need to be observed. However, many times the Spouse and Immediate Family Members may have some immediate expenditures to make in the preparation of Funeral Arrangements.

Some Family Members may need assistance coming to the Funeral. Additional food may need to be purchased, and certain other unforeseen expenditures may have to be made. Sometimes it may take several weeks before Insurance Policies may be processed and Benefits forwarded to the Beneficiary.

Bank Accounts that are solely on the Name of the Deceased should be left alone, for they are legally considered the Estate of Your Loved One. The legal processes of the **Probation of the Will** and/or the **Liquidation of the Estate** must be completed.

Safety Deposit Boxes - In many cases access to a **Safe Deposit Box** will be limited to a Family Member who is listed with the Bank Records, or to the legally confirmed **Executor**. In the event You have access, care should be taken to secure the necessary Document for addressing the immediate Business Affairs of Your Loved One.

Gathering Information

Investments - If Your Loved One had Investments of any kind, the Papers and Documents confirming the same should be kept in a safe place, and/or turned over to the **Executor**. In many cases a Beneficiary may be named. The Spouse may also be a Co-investor, in which case, the process should be begun to affirm the Death of Your Loved One, and the Investments subsequently listed in the name of the surviving Spouse, or other designees. In some cases certain Investments may need be liquidated in order to meet current financial obligations at hand.

Creditors/Outstanding Debts - Special care should be taken to assure the collection, itemization, and payment of **all** outstanding Bills and Debts of Your Loved One! In most cases the Bank Records, Cancelled Checks, and Receipts will reveal this information. However, various "**unknown**" Creditors may emerge as well. Usually the Executor will post Legal Notices in the Newspaper to address this concern

Credit Cards - Special care should be taken with Credit Cards. If they are in the name of the Deceased only, then as soon as is possible and feasible, those Debts should be paid off and the Cards **cancelled** to eliminate needless interest payments. If the Cards are also in the Spouse's name, then, upon liquidation of those Debts, there may be wisdom on the Spouse's part to **cancel** those specific cards and, if needed to secure a Card in their own name. This process would also help the Spouse establish or maintain Personal Credit Ratings. Many Female Spouses who have been Joint-tenants with their Husbands on Checking Accounts and Credit Cards are sadly surprised and hurt later when they seek loans on their own. **Destroy ALL Cancelled or Paid Off Credits Cards!**

Gathering Information

Tax Information - April 15th may be months away, but the Tax Information is another important matter to be addressed, even at this time. Tax Information reveals Sources of Income, Dependents, Investments, Business Obligations, and much, much more.

The Surviving Spouse will need to be aware of IRS regulations which may affect the subsequent Filing obligations, especially if the previous Tax Returns were filed separately. Care should also be taken to confirm whether the respective Insurance Benefits may be considered as taxable income to the Beneficiary, or not. The assistance of a Tax Consultant might be benficial at that time.

Mortgage Papers - Are you sure Momma is entitled to the House? Special care should be taken to review the Mortgage Papers, or even the Lease Agreement if renting. Copies of these Documents should be kept available and easily accessible.

The Surviving Spouse and Family should know exactly what their future Housing situation and obligations are and shall be in moments like this. Hopefully, proper transfer of Title to include the Spouse has already been finalized long before the Death of Your Loved One.

If not, then the House and any such Property will be included in the Decease's Estate, to be probated at a later time. This could prove to be a most disturbing matter for the Surviving Spouse and Family to face.

Military Records

If Your Loved One was a Member or former Member of the Armed Forces, then, in most cases, the **Military Records** will be kept in some readily available place.

Gathering Information

This information will be needed by the Funeral Home Staff to confirm any special privileges that Your Loved One and the Surviving Spouse and family Members may be entitled to. Be prepared to provide Your Loved One's **Serial Number, V.A. Claim Number,** and **G.I. Insurance Number.**

If in doubt, or if such information is not readily available, then contact should be made as soon as possible to the nearest Veterans Administration Office. Be aware that Certified Copies of the Death Certificate may be required for this Process.

Employer Information

Hopefully, Your Loved One was employed where certain Benefits were provided for moment such as this. Records and Documents should be available which specify various Benefits to which Your Loved One, Surviving Spouse, and Family are entitled. Contact should also be made to the present or former Employer(s) of Your Loved One, to inform them of Your Loved One's Death.

Be sure to seek confirmation of Your Loved One's **Retirement Information and Benefits; Pension Plans and Benefits; Group Life and Health Insurance Policies, Plans and Benefits; Accrued Vacation/Sick Pay; and any Credit Union Balances**. Be sure to seek in writing the procedures and persons responsible for processing this information and accessing any entitled Benefits. Be aware that Certified Copies of the Death Certificate may also be required for this Process.

Gathering Information

Personal Insurance Policies

Hopefully, the Insurance Policies of Your Loved One are readily accessible. In many cases knowing the name of the Insurance Company, and being able to provide the Social Security Number of the Deceased will enable the Insurance to search their Files to confirm the Policy of Your Loved One. It is best, however, to have original copies of the Policy when conversing with the Insurance Representative. Seek to confirm the Face Amount of the Policy (the base amount to be paid), and Dividends accrued (This might increase the total amount to be paid out.), the Beneficiaries, and the anticipated time to process the Death Claim. This might be crucial in determinig the method and time of paying the Funeral Expenses, and/or liquidating any outstanding Debts of Your Loved One. Be aware that Certified Copies of the Death Certificate may also be required for this Process.

Other Documents

You may run across some important and historical Documents and Papers which may not be needed for finalizing Your Loved One's Affairs, but they may prove to be most valuable for other Family Records and History. Try to catagorize them and keep them in a safe place for future reference.

Special Requests

Certain **Special Requests** may be considered with the **Final Instructions**, or included as part of the "**Last Will and Testament**". However, there may be some **Special Requests** that are Personal and are meant to be Expressions of Concern for various Family Members and Friends. Such **Requests** should be treated discreetly and shared privately with the Respective Person, unless other instructions are given. This may one of the last significant opportunities to Honor Your Loved One.

Chapter 6
Preparing for the Funeral

This process can be one of the most trying and frustrating portions of this experience if not planned and addressed properly. it is often in this phase that Family and Personal Feelings begin to surface. Care should be taken to assure, include, and address as many of these concerns as possible and feasible.

Counseling with the Pastor

Often the Pastor may be present at the time of Your Loved Ones Death. Since, under most cases, the Funeral Services will involve his Services and those of the Church to which Your Loved One belonged, his Advice and Counsel will be most invaluable. **Do not try to plan the Service without him!**

If there is a desire to include other Ministers, particularly those of the Family, be sure to secure the Pastor's approval before finalizing their assignment in the Service. This is especially important with certain Pastor's positions on women in the Service and in the Pulpit. Avoid arguing or insisting on any inclusions if the Pastor has objections. Remember, he has to continue his Ministry there long after the Family has returned to their homes and personal affairs. Respect his Convictions and Policies.

Confirming the Date & Time

Several factors may affect this decision. Not only must sufficient time be allowed for Family Members to get to the Funeral, but the schedule of the Funeral Home, the Pastor, and the Church at which the Services are to be held must be taken into consideration in order to confirm the Day of the Service. Sometimes the burial schedule of the Cemetery may also affect the time frame for the Funeral Service.

Preparing for the Funeral

Another factor for the choice of the Day and Time of Services is the work schedule of the Family Members planning to attend. Often Funerals held at the beginning or end of the week allow for Family Members to better adjust to work schedules.

Visitation With the Family

Prior to most Funeral Services a Designated Time is Scheduled to allow Friends of the Deceased to visit with the Family Members and personally express their Condolences. This period of time used to be termed as the **Wake** in some Cultural and Ethnic groups. While this Service may have been observed on the evening before the Funeral, primarily due to time constraints, more and more the Visitation time is often scheduled about an hour or so before the Funeral Service.

It has also proven to be more convenient and preferable by many Pastors to schedule Fraternal (Masonic, Eastern Star, etc.) or certain Community Group Ceremonies to be held during this time as well. This approach also allows the Funeral Service to focus more on the Biblical and Theological themes that need be addressed in behalf of Your Loved One.

Contacting Family Members

Care must be taken to inform as many Family Members as possible and feasible about the Funeral Plans. Contacting certain designated Members in given areas of the country and requesting them to contact other Family Members in their respective areas make facilitate this process, but also diminish telephone expenses.

Preparing for the Funeral

Writing the Obituary

The Obituary is one of the most important Documents in a Funeral. It is a brief history of the Deceased. It also serves as a synopsis of activities in which the Deceased was involved. (See Appendix.) Usually the local newspaper includes a daily section for Obituaries of persons who have died.

The Funeral Home Staff often facilitates getting the Obituary to the Newspaper. However, the Family is responsible for compiling the information.

The task of writing the Obituary should preferably be assigned to someone (Family Member or Friend) who has had previous experience doing so. Needless to say, many problems and disputes can be avoided by making sure that all information, name spellings and listings are accurate.

Selecting the Right Photograph(s)

Often the Newspapers will include a photograph of Your Loved One with the Obituary. You may also wish to have a Picture of Your Loved One on the Funeral Program. Depending upon the printing resources of the person responsible for printing the Program, separate photos may be needed for the Newspaper and the Program. Color photos may be used, but usually black and white photos are preferred. Try to select recent photos of Your Loved One for these purposes. Other photos may be used for a collage, or album, or video. These media are helpful as pictorial histories of Your Loved One. Often children, other Relatives, or even Friends, who are not aware of some of Your Loved One's many Life Experiences may be pleasantly surprised to see the same.

Preparing for the Funeral

Care should also be taken to avoid use of photos which may cause, or remind someone, of unpleasant Family experiences or Relationships (divorces, etc.)

Confirming Family Participants

Care should be taken in confirming with the designated Family Members who have been selected to Participate in the Funeral Service. Proper spelling of their names as well as designated functions and place in the Order of Service should also be confirmed with the person responsible for printing the Program. Remember to secure approval of their participation with the Pastor **before** confirming the same with them.

Selecting the Family Floral Spray

Usually, the Family will secure a **Family Floral Spray** to be placed on top of the Casket during the Service. The selection of Flowers for the Floral Spray should complement the color and the interior Lining of the Casket. Although the Funeral Home may facilitate the acquisition of the Floral Spray, be aware that this is an additional expense to the Family, and may be included in the Itemized Bill.

Memorial Tributes in Lieu of Flowers

Like it or not, the cost of these Floral Arrangements are continuing to increase. Also most of the Floral arrangements sent from various Family Members, Friends, and Organizations end up in the trash only hours after the Funeral. To compensate for these realities, many Families are encouraging that Special Contributions be made to designated Organizations or Charitable Institutions in Memory of their Loved One. To help assure compliance, these requests should be included in the Obituary information in the Newspaper, and also in the printed Funeral Program.

Preparing for the Funeral

Confirming the Family Assembly Place

Prior to proceding to the Church or Funeral Home for the Funeral, it is often helpful for the Family to assemble at a designated Family Member's Home. There any last minute instructions and plans can be acknowledged and clarified. Often this may be the home of the Deceased. There the Line Up of Cars can be confirmed. This also helps to confirm the needed Parking Space at the Church or Funeral Home for the Funeral.

Picking Up Arriving Family Members

Often some Family Members may be arriving by airline or train or bus and may need to be picked up upon arrival. Designating someone(s) to coordinate the Days and Times of these pick-ups will eliminate many undesired frustrations. This is also one of the important reasons for Informing Family Members of the Funeral Arrangement as soon as possible.

Confirming Lodging Arrangements

Depending upon the Housing arrangements of the Family Members living in the city where Your Loved One resided, Hotel or Motel Reservations may need be made. Care should be taken to be sure **who** will be responsible for paying for those **Rooms Reserved and Used**. Also be aware of the need for Handicap-Accessible rooms for Elderly Family Members.

Confirming Family Car Designations

Previous arrangements with the Funeral Home Staff should validate the number of Family Cars which would be needed. Usually the Funeral Home's Basic Services include at least one Family Car. Additional Cars may be available at additional cost. Keep these facts in mind as You address this matter.

Preparing for the Funeral

You will also want to Be aware of the following issues which need to be resolved:

Who Is To Ride In The Family Car(s)? Normally the Immediate Family Members would ride in the Main Family Car provided by the Funeral Home. The number of persons who can comfortably fit into the Main Family Car will give some direction as to who should be assigned to this vehicle. All other Family Members must be assigned to other Cars. Keep in mind that additional Family Cars **provided by the Funeral Home** will also result in additional Funeral Costs.

Who Will Be Driving The Other Cars? Care should be taken in the Assignment or Designation of Drivers for the Other Cars used for the rest of the Family Members. Strive to avoid assigning Persons who may be too emotionally distraught and those who have been drinking to be Drivers.

Who Will Be Riding in Which Car? Often Family Members driving from out of town will prefer to drive their own Cars. However, as much as is feasible, other Family Members riding in these Cars would help facilitate the Transportation matter. It may be helpful to develop a Listing of Family Members attending the Funeral and the Cars in which they each are riding.

Identifying the Funeral Cars

Special care should be taken for identifying the Cars participating in the Funeral Procession. In most cities the Funeral Home will provide magnetic flags to be placed on the hood of the car or adhesive signs to be placed in the front windshield. Additional caution is also taken by asking the drivers of the cars to turn on their headlights, as well as the flashing hazard lights.

Preparing for the Funeral

__Providing for Family Meals__

Sooner or later somebody is going to get hungry! When Family Members have gathered together in moments like these, often various Members of many Churches will bring covered dishes to feed the Bereaved Family. The Family should not assume, nor obligate the Church to perform this procedure. The initial obligation lies on the Family Members themselves.

However, whatever is provided by the Church Members ought be greatly appreciated and graciously accepted. Often the Church may plan to provide a meal for the Bereaved Family upon return of the Family from the Interment back to the Church. This procedure is quite helpful since some Family Members may need to drive back to their own hometowns following the Funeral. Family Members living in town may not feel up to the task of cooking for the rest of the Family Members.

__Proper Funeral Attire__

It is understood that Dressing habits and tastes may vary from Community to Community and Age Group to Age Group. However, it must also be kept in mind that there may be certain expectations for Dress in various Churches. Modesty should guide the choice of Clothing to be worn at the Funeral. Short skirts or dresses, revealing necklines and revealing splits in skirts or dresses, bare shoulders and mid-riffs are all **inappropriate** in a Funeral Service (or any Worship Service for that matter).

A dark suit for Men is proper. Hats and Caps are not usually accepted in most Sanctuaries. You should ask the Pastor to clarify the Church's Dress Code Policies. It should always be remembered that the Funeral Service is considered a **Worship Service**.

Preparing for the Funeral

Thus a "**Rule of Thumb**" should be for one to always present himself or herself in a respectful manner as if they were actually appearing before Almighty God Himself. Often the Funeral Service will direct the Bereaving Family's attention to the Lord's Guidance and Comfort in helping them to cope with the Death of their Loved One.

* * *

Chapter 7
Taking Care of Business

Almost immediately after the Death of Your Loved One, various Business Affairs must be addressed. Even before the Executor may begin his assigned responsibilities, certain Business matters may need be started. Usually the Will may clarify some of the responsibilities of the Executor. But in the event that the Spouse or another Family Member is left to handle the Affairs, the following are some matters to consider:

Contacting Legal Counsel

Sometimes the Deceased may have engaged in certain Business Deals or Arrangements with others of which the Spouse may have little or no knowledge. In such cases seeking Legal Advice may prove to be wise, especially since Tax Obligations may be involved. In the event that step-children are involved, Legal Counsel may be needed to clarify any Custody, Visitation, or Child-support obligations.

Contacting Banks/Financial Institutions

Access to needed Finances is a major concern. The nature and extent of any Financial Holdings will help determine which Financial Institutions to contact. Hopefully, records and copies of any Stocks, Bonds, or other Investments are accessible or easily retrieved. The Investment Firm ought be able to address these matters. The Spouse may need to utilize some of these Resources for the Funeral Expenses. Care should be taken, however, to seek second opinions about future Investments, as well as verifying any Beneficiaries of existing Investment Vehicles.

Taking Care of Business

Contacting the Social Security Office

If Your Loved One was covered under Social Security, then the Spouse is entitled to a lump sum Death Benefit. Application must be made within 12 months in order to receive it.

Be sure to report Your Loved One's Death to the Social Security Office as soon as possible. This may be an important factor in negotiating with the Funeral Home Staff for Services. In order to help process Your Loved One's Claim as soon as possible, be prepared to present the following Documents:

1. A Certified Copy of the Death Certificate.
2. Employment Information
   a. Employer's Name.
   b. Approximate Income during the year of Death.
   c. A Copy of the Insured's W-2 Form, if still working at the time of Death. (A Copy of the previous year's Tax Return will also be required.)
   d. Marriage Certificate and/or Divorce Decree.
   e. Proof of Age for each Surviving Dependent, including the Spouse and each Child.

Keep in mind also that, if Your Loved One was already receiving Social Security, then the receipt of a monthly check after his/her Death may present additional problems. That Check may have to be repaid.

Contacting the Veteran's Administration

If Your Loved One was a Veteran, contact with the Veteran's Administration will help determine any Benefits to which the Spouse and Surviving Dependents may be entitled. The VA Representatives should also inform You of a Burial Site and a Flag to drape the Casket.

Taking Care of Business

Contacting Insurance Companies

With Copies of the Insurance Policy(ies) or Certicifate(s) in hand, contact the Insurance Agent or Company. Be prepared to provide copies of the following Documents to settle the Claim:
1. A Certified Copy of the Death Certificate.
2. Policy or Certificate Number
3. Insured's Full Name and Address
4. Birth Certificate and/or Verification of the Insured's Date and Place of Birth.
5. Beneficiary(ies) Name(s) Address(es) and Social Security Number(s).

Paying Outstanding Debts

Just as important as paying the Funeral Expenses is the matter of Paying off all Outstanding Debts of Your Loved One. Sometimes this is not immediately feasible after the Funeral. Often some time will elapse before Social Security, VA, or Insurance Benefits are received. Resources in the Bank may not be adequate to accomplish this task either. In such cases, most Creditors are willing to accomodate the Spouse and make arrangements for Regular Payments to liquidate the Outstanding Debt.

Be sure to itemize each Outstanding Debt, the Amount Owed, the Amount to be Paid, and the Proposed Dates of Payment for each Person, Company, or Business to whom the Debt is Owed. **Be prompt in meeting these Obligations!**

Thanking Those Who Remembered

Usually the Funeral Home Staff will provide a Booklet in which the Visitors and Friends who attended the Funeral Services of Your Loved One can sign their Names and Addresses.

Taking Care of Business

This Information is most helpful in responding with **Thank You Notes**, or other Expressions of Appreciation, to those persons who responded to the Bereaved Family. Be sure to express the Family's Appreciation **in writing** as soon as possible also to those Persons, Friends, Family Members, Pastor, Church Staff, and others who responded to the Family with Floral Arrangements, Cards, Prayers, Monetary Contributions, Visitations, Advice, Encouragement, and any other Meaningful Expressions.

Providing for Those Who Remain

This is one area of Family Business that often gets pushed to the back burner. However, it should be one of the **Major Items** that is addressed, even before the Selection of the Casket is finalized!

When Your Loved One is in the Grave, and the Outstanding Debts have been addressed, some serious questions may still need to be answered. Where will the Surviving Spouse, Children and/or other Dependents be able to live? What Financial Resources are left to meet their ongoing needs? Will Health Care Service be needed for the Spouse or other Dependents? Which Family Member is available/willing to assume these Responsibilities?

Thorough investigation may need to be done in many of these areas in order to make the most Realistic and Practical Decisions. Ultimately, the "Buck" (and even "bucks/$$$") is going to stop at Someone's Feet, and some controversial and/or often questioned Decisions will have to be made. But the proper Care of the Surviving Spouse and Dependents must become the Major Priority!

Securing A Headstone Marker

One of the most important and yet often forgotten Business Matters is that of **Securing a Headstone Marker for Your Loved One**. Various references may be made during the Planning Stages of the Funeral, but in the rush of Family Members returning home after the Funeral, this matter may be left unaddressed.

Making this decision before those Immediate Family Members have left will help to save much time and frustration. A quick scanning of the Phonebook will indicate some of the Local Companies which render this service. It is wisdom to visit several Companies before finalizing your order. **Standing or Flat Headstones vary in price!** Be sure what type of Headstones are permitted in the Cemetery where Your Loved One is buried.

Also You should determine what the **specific wording** is to be engraved on the Headstone **before** You visit the various Companies. This will allow You to compare prices more accurately. Remember, **every** letter and punctuation mark costs something! The **Headstone Marker** is also part of the Funeral Costs.

* * *

"LORD, make me to know mine end, and the measure of my days, what it is; that I may know how frail I am."

- Psalm 39:4 (KJV)

Chapter 8
Facing the Future

When the Family Members have returned Home and back to Attending to their own Personal Affairs, some sobering Realities ought to come to **YOU**! Having seen the many issues that had to be addressed in behalf of Your Loved One, what if this had been You that other Family Members would have had to respond to? What Problems would they had had to encounter?

Now is the Time for You to Address these issues, and to ease the Burdens that Your Family will have to face when You Die!

Putting Your Own Affairs In Order

Take some Invaluable Time and start collecting Your Important Papers and Documents. Make Copies of them and keep the Originals and Copies in separate, but safe places. If You choose to place the Originals in a Safe Deposit Box at the Bank, be sure to keep up-to-date Copies in a safe place at Home. Organize Your Documents and Papers so that easy retrieval can be done when needed. Also, consider the following matters:

Keeping Your Will Updated

From time to time situations and circumstances may arise which may necessitate changing the Terms, Conditions, Executors, and/or Beneficiaries of Your Will. Do this as soon as possible and feasible under Legal Counsel.

Establishing a Pre-Arrangement Plan

More and more Family Situations are evolving where Spouses and Children are not in a position, nor condition, to carry the out the Arrangements for **YOUR** Funeral. In some cases existing Family Relationships may affect this decision.

Facing the Future

Many Persons are opting to establish **Pre-Arrangement Plans** in which many of the Decisions that had to be made for Your Loved One are made by the Individuals themselves.

Often many Funeral Homes are prepared to assist You in this Matter. With a **Pre-Arrangement Program** You can **select** Your Own Casket; **confirm** the Services that You want to be provided for Your Funeral; and **pay** for those Expenses prior to Your Demise. This approach will help to eliminate so many Emotional, Financial, and Procedural Problems at the time of Planning Your Funeral.

Keeping In Contact With Your Relatives

Often a Funeral becomes a major time for a Family Reunion. People who haven't seen each other in years will be brought together. Children who may have heard about Cousin "Lutie" or Uncle "Bud" finally get to see and meet them. In-laws are brought together. Newly-weds may have to confront the former Spouses. And all of this takes place under some strained circumstances.

To help diminish and/or eliminate much of these experiences for Your Loved Ones, strive to Personally keep in Contact with Your Relatives. Communicate frequently and regularly. (Family Reunions can help in this area also.) Above all, with all due respect to the evolving technology, take time to write, or at least make a Phone Call to Your Relatives. Encourage Your Children to do the same.

Keeping In Contact With Your Friends

The same efforts made for Your Relatives should also be made for Your Friends. Often Your Friends may be the first Persons who are able to come to Your Assistance in moments of need. When feasible and possible, encourage Your Children to know and communicate with Your Friends.

* * *

"Hear me speedily, O LORD:
my spirit faileth:
hide not thy face from me,
lest I be like unto them that go down into the pit.

Cause me to hear thy lovingkindness in the morning;
for in thee do I trust:
cause me to know the way wherein I should walk;
for I lift up my soul unto thee."

- Psalm 143:7,8 (KJV)

Chapter 9
Strengthening Your Spiritual Affairs

The Gospel Writer Matthew records Jesus saying, "*For what is a man profited, if he shall gain the whole world, and lose his own soul? or what shall a man give in exchange for his soul?" Matthew 16:26 (KJV).*

In this same perspective, what Benefit is it really for You to Master the Information in this Booklet; Get all of the Personal Affairs of Yourself and Your Loved Ones in Order, **and still not have Your Affairs with God in Order?!** Funerals are designed to bring People to Grips with the Reality of God's Plan for Salvation and Eternal Life. So as You read and enact the Information provided in this Booklet, the Challenge also comes to You to also **Strengthen Your Spiritual Affairs!** Hopefully, the following Information will help You do the same:

Reviewing Your Spiritual Life Style and Status

The Word of God makes the following Declarations that will reveal Your Spiritual Life Style and Status:

*"For all have sinned,
and come short of the glory of God..."
- Romans 3:23 (KJV)*

* * *

Strengthening Your Spiritual Affairs

"*For the wages of sin is death;*
but the gift of God is eternal life
through Jesus Christ our Lord."
- Romans 6:23 (KJV)

* * *

"*If we confess our sins,*
he is faithful and just to forgive us our sins,
and to cleanse us from all unrighteousness."
- I John 1:9 (KJV)

* * *

"*For God so loved the world,*
that he gave his only begotten Son,
that whosoever believeth in him should not perish,
but have everlasting life.
For God sent not his Son into the world
to condemn the world;
but that the world through him might be saved"
- John 3:16,17 (KJV)

* * *

"*Be it known unto you all,*
and to all the people of Israel,
that by the name of Jesus Christ of Nazareth,
whom ye crucified, whom God raised from the dead,
even by him doth this man
stand here before you whole.
Neither is there salvation in any other:
for there is none other name under heaven
given among men, whereby we must be saved."
- Acts 4:10,12 (KJV)

* * *

Strengthening Your Spiritual Affairs

"But God commendeth his love toward us, in that, while we were yet sinners, Christ died for us."
- Romans 5:8 (KJV)

* * *

*"That if thou shalt confess with thy mouth
the Lord Jesus,
and shalt believe in thine heart
that God hath raised him from the dead,
thou shalt be saved."
For with the heart man believeth unto righteousness;
and with the mouth confession
is made unto salvation."*
- Romans 10:9,10 (KJV)

* * *

*"Therefore if any man be in Christ,
he is a new creature:
old things are passed away;
behold, all things are become new."*
- 2 Corinthians 5:17 (KJV)

* * *

*"For as in Adam all die,
even so in Christ shall all be made alive."*
- 1 Corinthians 15:22 (KJV)

* * *

*"I am crucified with Christ: nevertheless I live;
yet not I, but Christ liveth in me:
and the life which I now live in the flesh*

Strengthening Your Spiritual Affairs

I live by the faith of the Son of God, who loved me, and gave himself for me."
- Galatians 2:20 (KJV)

* * *

Setting Your House In Order

"In those days was Hezekiah sick unto death. And the prophet Isaiah the son of Amoz came to him, and said unto him, Thus saith the LORD, Set thine house in order; for thou shalt die, and not live."
- II Kings 20:1 (KJV)

* * *

"Whereas ye know not what shall be on the morrow. For what is your life? It is even a vapour, that appeareth for a little time, and then vanisheth away."
- James 4:14 (KJV)

* * *

"For I am now ready to be offered, and the time of my departure is at hand. I have fought a good fight, I have finished my course, I have kept the faith:

Henceforth there is laid up for me a crown of righteousness, which the Lord, the righteous judge, shall give me at that day: and not to me only, but unto all them also that love his appearing."
- 2 Timothy 4:6-8 (KJV)

* * *

Strengthening Your Spiritual Affairs

"And as it is appointed unto men once to die, but after this the judgment:"
- Hebrews 9:27 (KJV)

* * *

No doubt after reading these Passages of Scripture, God's Word has spoken to You. And as the Holy Spirit Convicts You of the Truth of these Words, and Guides You to follow Them in Your Heart, You will Experience a greater Desire for Spiritual Change and Growth in Your Life.

You will also find that Continued Bible Study, Sincere Prayer, Regular Worship, Genuine Fellowship with Believers in Christ Jesus, and Faithful Service to the Kingdom of God will all be great **Sources and Resources for Your Spiritual Strength**. Follow these Faithfully, and You will find Yourself **Strengthening Your Spiritual Affairs and Getting Your House in Order!**

* * *

My Prayer

Almighty God, Look down and Hear My Prayer today.
    Please Touch my Heart and Wash my Sins away.
Open my Eyes, O Lord, that I might ever See
    Glimpses of Truth that Thou hast Need of Me.

Then Guide My Feet along Life's Pathway Everyday;
    Lead through the Stones and Thorns along the Way.
Then Use My Tongue to Speak Thy Word to Every Man.
    And Let Thy Love Be Shown through Mine own Hand.

Forgive Me, Lord, for All the Sins that Stain My Heart:
    The Lust, the Greed that Tears My Soul apart.
Purge out the Sins that Swell within My Selfish Pride,
    That I might Know, in Thee, I'm Purified.

Lord, Bear My Soul thru all the Flames of Patience's Fires;
    Transform My Mind to Seek What Thou Desire.
Redeem My Life that I might Live on One Accord
    With Fellowmen, and always with My Lord.

Bless then, O Lord, My Brother who in earnest tries
    To Cause some Gleam to Fall within Mine Eyes.
And Let My Life a Faith Profession ever be,
    Conquering Sin on Battlefields for Thee.

And when the Trumpet Calls My Weary Soul to rest;
    Grant then, O Lord, a Rank among the Blest.
Then Rock My Soul within the Cradle of Thy Love;
    And Feed Me with the Manna from Above.

        - Samuel W. Hale, Jr.

Chapter 10
Other Scriptures For These Moments

One of the most effective sources of Comfort at the Death of Your Loved One is the Bible, the Word of God. It is in in those Moments of Stillness and Uncertainty that God's Word can bring Comfort, Hope, and Peace to Your Soul. You might share the following passages of Scripture with Your Family Members and Friends for Spiritual Guidance and Reassurance.

The Biblical View of Death

"Now this I say, brethren, that flesh and blood cannot inherit the kingdom of God; neither doth corruption inherit incorruption.

Behold, I shew you a mystery; We shall not all sleep, but we shall all be changed, In a moment, in the twinkling of an eye, at the last trump: for the trumpet shall sound, and the dead shall be raised incorruptible, and we shall be changed.

For this corruptible must put on incorruption, and this mortal must put on immortality.

So when this corruptible shall have put on incorruption, and this mortal shall have put on immortality, then shall be brought to pass the saying that is written, Death is swallowed up in victory.

O death, where is thy sting? O grave, where is thy victory?

Other Scriptures For These Moments

The sting of death is sin; and the strength of sin is the law. But thanks be to God, which giveth us the victory through our Lord Jesus Christ.

Therefore, my beloved brethren, be ye stedfast, unmoveable, always abounding in the work of the Lord, forasmuch as ye know that your labour is not in vain in the Lord."
- 1 Cor 15:50-57 (KJV)

* * *

"But I would not have you to be ignorant, brethren, concerning them which are asleep, that ye sorrow not, even as others which have no hope.

For if we believe that Jesus died and rose again, even so them also which sleep in Jesus will God bring with him. For this we say unto you by the word of the Lord, that we which are alive and remain unto the coming of the Lord shall not prevent them which are asleep.

For the Lord himself shall descend from heaven with a shout, with the voice of the archangel, and with the trump of God: and the dead in Christ shall rise first:

Then we which are alive and remain shall be caught up together with them in the clouds, to meet the Lord in the air: and so shall we ever be with the Lord.

Wherefore comfort one another with these words."
- 1 Thessalonians 4:13-18 (KJV)

Other Scriptures For These Moments

God's Assurance for Your Strength

"For I know that thou wilt bring me to death, and to the house appointed for all living."
- Job 30:23 (KJV)

* * *

"Yea, though I walk through the valley of the shadow of death, I will fear no evil: for thou art with me; thy rod and thy staff they comfort me."
- Psalm 23:4 (KJV)

* * *

"I will lift up mine eyes unto the hills, from whence cometh my help. My help cometh from the LORD, which made heaven and earth. He will not suffer thy foot to be moved: he that keepeth thee will not slumber. Behold, he that keepeth Israel shall neither slumber nor sleep.

The LORD is thy keeper: the LORD is thy shade upon thy right hand. The sun shall not smite thee by day, nor the moon by night.

The LORD shall preserve thee from all evil: he shall preserve thy soul. The LORD shall preserve thy going out and thy coming in from this time forth, and even for evermore."
- Psalm 121 (KJV)

* * *

Other Scriptures For These Moments

"Mark the perfect man, and behold the upright: for the end of that man is peace."
- Psalm 37:37

* * *

The Best Is Yet To Come

"For now should I have lain still and been quiet, I should have slept: then had I been at rest, With kings and counsellors of the earth, which built desolate places for themselves; Or with princes that had gold, who filled their houses with silver: Or as an hidden untimely birth I had not been; as infants which never saw light.

There the wicked cease from troubling; and there the weary be at rest. There the prisoners rest together; they hear not the voice of the oppressor. The small and great are there; and the servant is free from his master."
- Job 3:13-19 (KJV)

* * *

"Then shall the King say unto them on his right hand, Come, ye blessed of my Father, inherit the kingdom prepared for you from the foundation of the world:"
- Matthew 25:34 (KJV)

* * *

Other Scriptures For These Moments

"And Jesus said unto him, Verily I say unto thee, To day shalt thou be with me in paradise."
- Luke 23:43 (KJV)

* * *

"Jesus said unto her, I am the resurrection, and the life: he that believeth in me, though he were dead, yet shall he live: And whosoever liveth and believeth in me shall never die. Believest thou this?"
- John 11:25,26 (KJV)

* * *

"In my Father's house are many mansions: if it were not so, I would have told you. I go to prepare a place for you. And if I go and prepare a place for you, I will come again, and receive you unto myself; that where I am, there ye may be also."
- John 14:2,3 (KJV)

* * *

"And as we have borne the image of the earthy, we shall also bear the image of the heavenly."
- 1 Corinthians 15:49 (KJV)

* * *

"For we know that if our earthly house of this tabernacle were dissolved, we have a building of God, an house not made with hands, eternal in the heavens."
- 2 Corinthians 5:1 (KJV)

* * *

Other Scriptures For These Moments

"And I heard a voice from heaven saying unto me, Write, Blessed are the dead which die in the Lord from henceforth: Yea, saith the Spirit, that they may rest from their labours; and their works do follow them."
- Revelation 14:13 (KJV)

* * *

"After this I beheld, and, lo, a great multitude, which no man could number, of all nations, and kindreds, and people, and tongues, stood before the throne, and before the Lamb, clothed with white robes, and palms in their hands; And cried with a loud voice, saying, Salvation to our God which sitteth upon the throne, and unto the Lamb.

And all the angels stood round about the throne, and about the elders and the four beasts, and fell before the throne on their faces, and worshipped God, Saying, Amen: Blessing, and glory, and wisdom, and thanksgiving, and honour, and power, and might, be unto our God for ever and ever. Amen.

And one of the elders answered, saying unto me, What are these which are arrayed in white robes? and whence came they? And I said unto him, Sir, thou knowest. And he said to me, These are they which came out of great tribulation, and have washed their robes, and made them white in the blood of the Lamb.

Therefore are they before the throne of God, and serve him day and night in his temple: and he that sitteth on the throne shall dwell among them.

Other Scriptures For These Moments

They shall hunger no more, neither thirst any more; neither shall the sun light on them, nor any heat. For the Lamb which is in the midst of the throne shall feed them, and shall lead them unto living fountains of waters: and God shall wipe away all tears from their eyes."
  - Revelation 7:9 -17 (KJV)

# # #

BECAUSE OF ME

Because of Me My Savior died -
   On Calv'ry's Cross was Crucified.
The Price of Sin for Me was Paid -
   By His Own Blood My Death was Stayed.
Because of Me Creation Cried -
   The Sun behind the Clouds did Hide;
The Morning Stars in Sorrow Sang -
   The Earth replied in Solemn Strain.

Because of Me in Joseph's Tomb
   My Lord was Laid to Change My Doom.
In Darkness all Alone He Stayed -
   My Ransom Price of Death was Paid.
Because of Me - that Sunday Morn -
   The Grave was Burst - Asunder Torn;
The Grip of Death was Paralyzed.
   To Eternal Shores My Soul Shall Rise!

Because of Me Christ Shall Return!
   His Face Mine Eyes shall Soon Discern.
Through Cloven Skies He Shall descend
   And Rapture Me and You, My Friend!
Because of Me Dear Calv'ry's Lamb
   Prepared a Feast - a Guest I Am.
With Saints Who have through Fires been Tried,
   We'll All Sit Down - the Savior's Bride!

O Praise His Name, Who, Free from Guile,
   Forgave My Sins - Made Me His Child;
Redeemed My Soul and Set Me free,
   And Shared His Love Eternally.
Praise Him, My Soul, for I have Found
   My Name is also Written Down
Inside His Book of Life, You See -
   He Did It All Because of Me!

      - Samuel W. Hale, Jr.

Appendices

The following pages may be photocopied for personal use.

OBITUARY FORMAT

The Obituary is actually a synopsis of the Life of the Deceased. It seeks to accquaint and/or remind the Reader about the Deceased. Writing the Obituary can be a most challenging experience, especially for those Family Members for whom this will be their first time. Who is suppose to write it? What do you say? What all should go into it? How should you begin? What do you do with it? How does it get in the newspaper? What role does the Funeral Home have in it?

All, and each, of these questions can become mountains within themselves if not answered properly. But when written properly, the Life of Your Loved One can be presented in a manner which is factual and interesting. Since Obituaries are often used for Historical Record, it is very important to make sure that all Names, Places, and Dates are accurate. The Name of the Surviving Wife should include the Maiden Name. This is beneficial for Family History purposes. The Names of the other Spouses in the Family might be placed in parentheses ( ) in the listing of other Relatives.

The Following Sample Obituary Guide should help to answer many of these questions:

* * *

OBITUARY
for
(Name of Deceased)

* * *

Selected Scripture or Short Poem
(Optional)

* * *

(Name of Deceased) was born in (Place of Birth) on (Date of Birth) to the Union of (Name of Father and Mother). He/She married (Name Spouse, using Maiden Name of Wife). To this Union was born (Name the Children of this Marriage. Acknowledge any Adopted Children also).

He/She grew up in (Location) and attended Public School in (Location, if different). He/She furthered His/Her education at (Name of College or University) receiving the (Name and Focus of Degree[s]).

(Name of Deceased) was employed as a (Job Title) at the (Name of Employer) for (Length of Employment). He/She also was a Member of the (Name[s] of various Organizations, Groups, to which the Deceased belonged).

In (Appropriate Year) (Name of Deceased) united with the (Name of Church) and served as (Name the Positions and/or Functions and the respective length of time in which the Deceased served).

On (Day and Date of Death) God Called (Name of Deceased) Home. (A statement about the circumstances of the Deceased's Health Situation may be added, if desired.) He/She leaves to mourn His/Her passing (Identify the Family Members, their Spouses, and their Places of Residence in the following order):

OBITUARY FORMAT

1. Surviving Spouse
2. Children of Surviving Spouse
3. Other Children, if applicable
4. Grand/Great-grand Children
5. Parents, if Living
6. Siblings
7. Nieces/Nephews/Cousins

* * *

Selected Scripture or Short Poem (Optional)

# # #

PERSONAL INFORMATION INVENTORY

Part I - Personal Information

Name: _____ Phone: _____

Address: _____

Date of Birth ___/___/___

Place of Birth_____

Social Security # ___/___/___ Medicare I.D #_____

Location of Important Papers/Documents

Birth Certificate   _____

Marriage Certificate   _____

Divorce Decree   _____

Adoption Papers   _____

Military Records   _____
    Serial #   _____
    V.A. Claim #   _____
    G.I. Insurance #   _____

Fraternal Burial Records   _____
    Serial #   _____

Mortgage Papers   _____

Real Estate Deeds   _____

Pre-Arrangement Papers   _____

Cemetery Plot Deeds   _____

Tax Records   _____

Will   _____

Special Persons to Contact

Will Prepared By:

    Name _____

    Address _____

    Phone _____

Executor of Estate:

    Name _____

    Address _____

    Phone _____

Attorney:

    Name _____

    Address _____

    Phone _____

Other:

    Name _____

    Address _____

    Phone _____

Other:

    Name _____

    Address _____

    Phone _____

Other:

    Name _____

    Address _____

    Phone _____

Part II - Financial Information

Bank Accounts

Location _____

   __ Joint   __ Individual

   Checking Account # _____

   Saving Account # _____

   Other Account # _____

   Lock Box # _____

Location _____

   __ Joint   __ Individual

   Checking Account # _____

   Saving Account # _____

   Other Account # _____

   Lock Box # _____

Location _____

   __ Joint   __ Individual

   Checking Account # _____

   Saving Account # _____

   Other Account # _____

   Lock Box # _____

Investments - Securities, Stocks, Bonds, Certificates of Deposit, Money Market Accounts, etc.

Type: _____

Location _____

   __ Joint   __ Individual

   Account # _____

   Agent _____

   Address _____

   Phone _____

Type: _____

Location _____

   __ Joint   __ Individual

   Account # _____

   Agent _____

   Address _____

   Phone _____

Type: _____

Location _____

   __ Joint   __ Individual

   Account # _____

   Agent _____

   Address _____

   Phone _____

Retirement/Pension Benefits

Type: _____

    Account # _____

    Company _____

    Address _____

    Phone _____

    Beneficiary _____

Type: _____

    Account # _____

    Company _____

    Address _____

    Phone _____

    Beneficiary _____

Other Income

Type: _____

    __ Joint   __ Individual

    Account # _____

    Company _____

    Address _____

    Phone _____

    Beneficiary _____

Outstanding Loans and Debts

Type: _____

   Owed to: _____

   Balance Due $_____

   Location of Documents _____

Type: _____

   Owed to: _____

   Balance Due $_____

   Location of Documents _____

Type: _____

   Owed to: _____

   Balance Due $_____

   Location of Documents _____

Credit Card Debts

Type Card: _____

   Account # _____

   Phone _____

   Balance Due $_____

Type Card: _____

   Account # _____

   Phone _____

   Balance Due $_____

Credit Card Debts (Continued)

Type Card: _____

    Account # _____

    Phone _____

    Balance Due $_____

Type Card: _____

    Account # _____

    Phone _____

    Balance Due $_____

Type Card: _____

    Account # _____

    Phone _____

    Balance Due $_____

Type Card: _____

    Account # _____

    Phone _____

    Balance Due $_____

Type Card: _____

    Account # _____

    Phone _____

    Balance Due $_____

Health Insurance Policy

__ Group __ Individual

Policy/Certificate # _____

Company _____

Address _____

_____

Phone _____

Type of Coverage _____

Face Amount $_____ Deductible $_____

Agent's Name _____ Phone _____

Location of Policy _____

Life Insurance Policy

__ Group __ Individual

Policy/Certificate # _____

Company _____

Address _____

_____

Phone _____

Type of Coverage _____

Face Amount $_____ Deductible $_____

Agent's Name _____ Phone _____

Location of Policy _____

Life Insurance Policy

__ Group __ Individual

Policy/Certificate #_____

Company _____

Address _____

_____

Phone _____

Type of Coverage _____

Face Amount $_____ Deductible $_____

Agent's Name_____ Phone _____

Location of Policy_____

Home Insurance Policy

Policy/Certificate #_____

Company _____

Address _____

_____

Phone _____

Type of Coverage _____

Face Amount $_____ Deductible $_____

Agent's Name_____ Phone _____

Location of Policy_____

Auto Insurance Policy

Policy/Certificate # _____

Company _____

Address _____
_____

Phone _____

Type of Coverage _____

Car(s) Covered _____
_____

Face Amount $_____ Deductible $_____

Agent's Name_____ Phone _____

Location of Policy_____

Long-Term Care Policy

Policy/Certificate # _____

Company _____

Address _____
_____

Phone _____

Type of Coverage _____

Face Amount $_____ Deductible $_____

Agent's Name_____ Phone _____

Location of Policy_____

Other Insurance Policies

Policy/Certificate #_____

Company _____

Address _____

_____

Phone _____

Type of Coverage _____

Face Amount $_____ Deductible $_____

Agent's Name_____ Phone _____

Location of Policy_____

* * *

Policy/Certificate #_____

Company _____

Address _____

_____

Phone _____

Type of Coverage _____

Face Amount $_____ Deductible $_____

Agent's Name_____ Phone _____

Location of Policy_____

THE FAMILY SEATING ORDER

This event can become one of the most serious moments that may affect Family Relationships and Feelings for years to come. Care should be taken to respect the health conditions particularly of Elderly Family Members. Their ability to walk long distances should be taken under consideration in Car Assignments.

The following Seating Orders should be observed as much as is feasible for the respective situations:

Funeral Car(s) - From Family Home
1. Surviving Spouse
2. Children of Surviving Spouse
3. Other Children, if applicable

Family Car(s)
1. Parents, if Living
2. Grand/Great-grand Children
3. Siblings
4. Nieces/Nephews/Cousins
5. In-Laws not Riding with their Spouses

At the Funeral
1. Surviving Spouse
2. Children of Surviving Spouse
3. Other Children if Present
4. Parents/Grand-Parents if Present
5. Grand/Great-grand Children
6. Siblings
7. Nieces/Nephews/Cousins
8. In-Laws not Sitting with their Spouses

Funeral Procession - From the Church or Funeral Home to the Cemetery

1. Lead Funeral Car (Funeral Home Staff)
2. Pastor
3. Pall Bearers
4. Hearse
5. **Funeral Cars**
6. **Family Cars**
7. Friends
8. Others Going to Cemetery

# # #

FUNERAL HOME SERVICE CHARGES

Special care should be taken to be extremely clear on this matter. Before You begin talking about Your Choice of a Casket, or even about Funeral Arrangements, **ask the Funeral Home Staff to SHOW You and those Family Members with You an Itemized Copy of their Services!**

Take special note of the following Items:
The Basic Service Costs	$_____
(What all is included in these Services?)	
The Cost for Family Cars	$_____
The Cost of the Casket	$_____
The Cost for Opening/Closing the Grave	$_____
The Cost and Procedures for Cremation	$_____
The Cost for Beautician Services	$_____
The Cost for the Burial Vaults	$_____
The Honorium for the Minister/Musician	$_____
Other Charges	$_____
TOTAL	**$_____**

Wisdom suggests that this type of Information be thought about and secured **prior** to such situations when You are directly involved. In some situations Your Pastor may be aware of some of these Costs. It is not improper to inquire of this Information from Funeral Homes to **compare prices** from time to time. Remember, Funeral Homes are still **Businesses**, and Your Family is still expected to pay for the Services that You secure from them.

# # #

FUNERAL PLANNING CHECK LIST

Use this Check List to help You keep account of the various Tasks, Responsibilities, and Persons Responsible for doing these various Tasks in Planning the Funeral Arrangements for Your Loved One.

Persons to Contact
- __ The Immediate Family
- __ The Pastor
- __ The Funeral Home Staff
- __ The Doctor
- __ The Rest of the Family and Friends
- __ Arrange for an Autopsy (If Needed)
- __ Other _____

Special Meetings
- __ Meet with the Pastor
    - __ Confirm Funeral Date and Time
    - __ Confirm Special Requests for the Funeral Service
    - __ Confirm the Family Participants in the Service
    - __ Other _____
- __ Meet with the Funeral Home Staff
    - __ Confirm Funeral Date and Time
    - __ Select Casket
    - __ Confirm Funeral Services and Expenses
    - __ Confirm Payment Arrangements
    - __ Secure Certified Copies of the Death Certificate
    - __ Other _____
- __ Meet with Legal Counsel
    - __ Confirm a Will
    - __ Affirm the Executor of the Estate
    - __ Clarify Legal Procedures and Obligations
    - __ Other _____

FUNERAL PLANNING CHECK LIST (Continued)

Family Decisions to be Made
- [ ] Confirm Family Assembly Place
- [ ] Confirm Meal Arrangements
- [ ] Confirm Lodging Arrangements
- [ ] Who will Write the Obituary?
- [ ] Select the Photos
- [ ] Select the Funeral Spray
- [ ] Pick Up Family Members
- [ ] Confirm Family Car Designations
- [ ] Who will Handle the Business Affairs?
- [ ] Who Needs Assistance to the Funeral?
- [ ] How will They get There?
- [ ] Selecting a Headstone Marker

Business Affairs to be Addressed
- [ ] Is there a Will? Where is it Located?
- [ ] What Financial Resources are readily Accessible? Where?
- [ ] Who has Access? _____
- [ ] Where are the other Important Papers, Bills, Documents? _____
- [ ] What Bills Need Immediate Attention?
- [ ] Contact Insurance Companies
- [ ] Contact Employers
- [ ] Contact Veterans Administration
- [ ] Contact Social Security Office
- [ ] Make Arrangements for Care of Surviving Spouse/Children
- [ ] _____

* * *

SUGGESTED ORDERS OF SERVICE

At The Church or Funeral Home

Visitation With The Family

* * *

Meditation in Music

* * *

Call to Worship
Hymn of Affirmation (Congregation)
Invocation
Selected Scriptures

* * *

Special Music (Choir or Solo)

* * *

Tribute(s) to the Deceased
Acknowledgments, Resolutions
Words of Comfort - Clergy

* * *

Special Music (Choir or Solo)

* * *

Eulogy/Message
Moments of Reflection
Recessional Sentences

* * *

Depart for the Interment

# # #

The Benediction is normally given at the Gravesite.

SUGGESTED ORDERS OF SERVICE
(Continued)

At The Gravesite

Opening Sentences (Minister)
Invocation
Selected Scriptures

* * *

Words of Comfort - Clergy

* * *

Eulogy/Message
Moments of Reflection
Benediction

* * *

Depart for Family Gathering

\# \# \#

SPECIAL NOTES

Wakes/Visitation With The Family - Many Churches and Families no longer hold the **Wake** on the Evening preceding the Funeral on the next day. Instead, the Body of the Deceased may lie in state one to two hours prior to the Funeral. Approximately one hour before the Funeral the Family may arrive for Private or Public Viewing of Their Loved One before the Funeral. Friends and Loved Ones usually take this time to view the Body and express Condolences to the Family.

Sometimes the Family may request a **Private Viewing** of their Loved One. This should be done, either at the Funeral Home on the day preceding the Funeral, or at the Church or Funeral Home prior to the Public Viewing.

SPECIAL NOTES (Continued)

Some Churches still hold the Funeral Services in the Evening. This approach allows Family and Friends who are traveling long distance to leave early the next morning. It also allows the Family Members to rest emotionally as well as physically following the Funeral Services. This approach may, however, create some inconveniences in planning moments of Fellowship following the Committal Services at the Cemetery.

Memorial Observations of Fraternal Organizations - In the event that Your Loved One was a Member of a Fraternal Organization, the Family may desire that Group to perform their Memorial Observations in behalf of Your Loved One. In keeping with the Biblical Principles of Life and Death, such Memorial Observations should occur at the **close** of the **Visitation With The Family** period and **PRIOR** to the beginning of the Funeral Service itself.

It must be remembered that the **Funeral Service** is designed and intended to encourage the Family and Friends to focus on their Loved One's Relationship to the Lord and to remind them of His Love and Strength and Comfort in their moments of Bereavement.

With all due respect to the Fraternal Organizations, the **Church** and the **Minister** are the **Official Representatives of God**. Thus **all** aspects of the **Funeral Service** should be finalized and directed by the **Pastor** or **Minister in Charge**.

Military Ceremonies - In the event that Your Loved One was a **Veteran**, and when the Committal of the Body is done in a Military Cemetery, it may be customary for a Military Detail of Veterans to perform **Military Ceremonies**. In such case, the **Military Ceremony** should also **PRECEDE** the **Committal Services** performed by the Pastor or Minister in Charge. Regardless of the significance of Your Loved One's Military Record, the Lord has the **Last Word** for Your Loved One!